# WOMAN TO WOMAN STUDY GUIDE

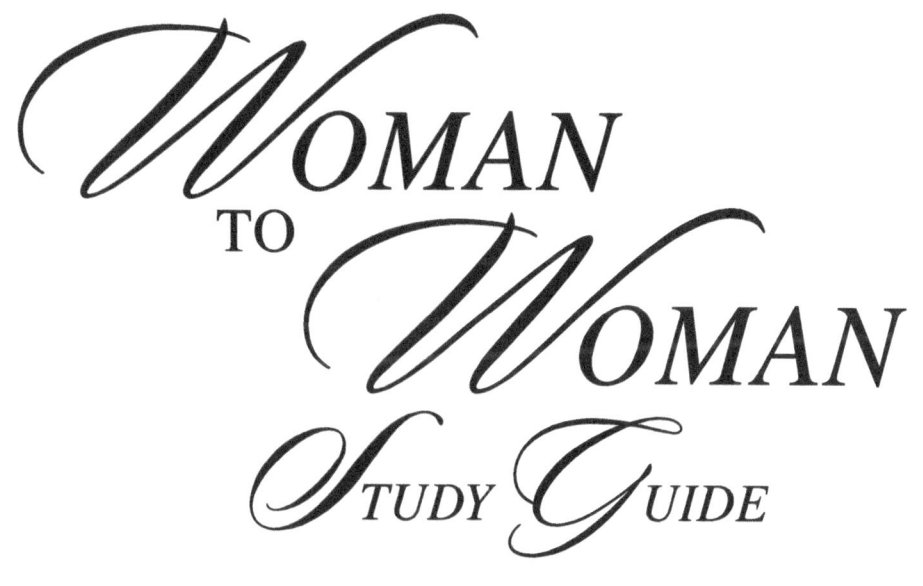

Unleashing The Power of
Intergenerational Mentorship

**RACHAEL & VALERIA**
**EDMONDS**

# Table of Contents

**Introduction** — 1
Overview of Woman to Woman: The Power of
Intergenerational Mentorship — 2
How to Use This Study Guide — 3

**Session 1** — 7
The Power of Relationship

**Session 2** — 11
Walking Through Life's Transitions Together

**Session 3** — 15
Seeking Wise Counsel

**Session 4** — 19
Mentorship in Action

**Session 5** — 23
The Rewards of Mentorship

**Session 6** — 27
Becoming Women Who Lift as We Rise

**Final Words** — 33
You Are Part of God's Greater Story

**Appendix** — 35
Intergenerational Mentoring Case Study

# Introduction

Our lives as women are shaped by relationships, wisdom, and the guidance of those who have walked before us. Throughout history, women have gained strength from one another, passing down knowledge, faith, and encouragement across generations. Intergenerational mentorship is essential because it provides support, guidance, and wisdom for navigating life's complexities.

The Apostle Paul instructed older women to teach and encourage younger women (Titus 2:3-5), showing that mentorship is a biblical principle that strengthens individuals, families, and communities. Whether it's in faith, relationships, career, or personal growth, every woman benefits from the wisdom of another who has walked ahead.

Yet, mentorship is not just about receiving—it's about giving back. As we learn from those ahead of us, we must also be willing to invest in those coming behind us. This cycle of learning and leading ensures that each generation is stronger, wiser, and better equipped for life's challenges.

## Overview of Woman to Woman: The Power of Intergenerational Mentorship

This study guide is a companion to Woman to Woman: The Power of Intergenerational Mentorship, a book that explores the unique challenges, experiences, and wisdom of women at different life stages. The book highlights real-life stories, biblical principles, and practical guidance for mentoring across generations.

In *Woman to Woman*, each chapter provides insight into what women in different age groups experience, with advice from older women who have already navigated those seasons. Some of the key themes include:

- **Embracing change and transitions** (20s-30s)
- **Balancing career, relationships, and faith** (30s-40s)
- **Finding purpose and legacy** (50s-60s)

The book reminds us that women are meant to walk through life together—encouraging, teaching, and uplifting one another. It calls us to be both students and teachers, always learning and always sharing wisdom.

*Chapter 8: A Mentoring Guide* reinforces the value of mentoring and provides a framework for intentional mentorship, helping women understand:

- **How to find and build mentoring relationships**
- **How to be a mentor and a mentee at the same time**
- **The power of shared experiences and storytelling**

This study guide expands on those lessons by connecting them to one of the most beautiful examples of mentorship in the Bible—the relationship between Naomi and Ruth.

## How to Use This Study Guide

This study guide is designed to:

- ☑ **Deepen your understanding** of the importance of mentorship
- ☑ **Connect biblical wisdom to modern mentorship** through Naomi and Ruth's story
- ☑ **Encourage self-reflection** on where you need guidance and where you can give it
- ☑ **Provide practical steps** for starting and maintaining meaningful mentoring relationships

Each session will explore a part of Naomi and Ruth's journey, connecting it to themes from *Woman to Woman: The Power of Intergenerational Mentorship*. You will be challenged to embrace mentorship as both a receiver and a giver of wisdom through discussion, reflection, prayer, and action steps. Here's how…

## 💡 For Individual Study:

- Read each session and reflect on the discussion questions.
- Review the chapter in the book that relates to your mentor or mentee
- Journal your thoughts and action steps.
- Pray for wisdom in mentorship relationships.

## 💡 For Group Study:

- Ask women of different ages to read the chapter of the book, *Woman to Woman*, that relates to their stage in life and invite them to a group study
- Gather with the women for weekly sessions.

- Read the scripture passage together during each session.
- Review the key themes as a group
- Use the discussion questions to share experiences and insights.
- Commit to supporting one another beyond the study.

## 💡 For One-on-One Mentorship:

- Meet regularly with a mentor or mentee.
- Review the chapter in the book, *Woman to Woman*, that relates to your mentor or mentee.
- Go through each session and discuss how it applies to your lives.
- Use the action steps to **intentionally grow together**.

INTRODUCTION

## *A Prayer for Mentorship & This Study*

**Heavenly Father,**

*Thank You for the gift of mentorship and for the women You place in our lives to guide, encourage, and support us. Just as You worked through Naomi and Ruth, I ask that You bring meaningful mentorship relationships into my life.*

If I need wisdom, lead me to a godly mentor who can help me navigate life's challenges.

If I have wisdom to share, open my heart to pour into others with grace and humility.

Help me to trust You in every season, knowing that my experiences—both good and bad—can be used to strengthen and uplift others.

May this study draw me closer to You, Lord, and help me build relationships that reflect Your love, wisdom, and purpose.

In Jesus' name,

**Amen.**

# Session 1

## *The Power of Relationship*

### Learning from Naomi and Ruth

**Scripture Focus:**

**Ruth 1:1-18** *(Read aloud or reflect on this passage)*

*"But Ruth replied, 'Don't urge me to leave you or to turn back from you. Where you go, I will go, and where you stay, I will stay. Your people will be my people and your God my God.'"*

— Ruth 1:16 (NIV)

### Key Themes:

- **The Strength of Mentorship Through Relationship:** Naomi and Ruth's bond shows that mentorship isn't just about knowledge—it's about love, commitment, and walking through life together.

- **The Role of Shared Life Experiences:** Naomi and Ruth had both experienced loss, which deepened their connection. Shared struggles often form the foundation for strong mentoring relationships.
- **The Importance of Choosing a Mentor or Mentee Wisely:** Ruth chose to follow Naomi not only because of their relationship but also because of Naomi's wisdom and faith.

## Connection to *Woman to Woman*

In *Chapter 8: A Mentoring Guide*, the book emphasizes that mentorship is built on **intentionality, trust, and mutual growth**. Just like Naomi did not actively seek to mentor Ruth, many of the best mentoring relationships happen organically. *The book advises women to be open to both receiving and giving mentorship*, understanding that sometimes the best guidance comes from unexpected places.

Additionally, the wisdom from older women in each chapter reflects the *importance of intergenerational relationships*. For example, women in their fifties advised younger women:

*"Surround yourself with people who bring you wisdom, not just company."*

Naomi's wisdom made her the kind of woman Ruth could trust with her future.

## Reflection & Discussion Questions

1. **What qualities made Naomi a mentor worth following?** What qualities did Ruth show that made her a teachable and faithful mentee?
2. **Have you ever had a "Naomi" in your life?** Reflect on a woman who has guided you through life's challenges. What impact did she have on you?
3. **Why do you think Ruth was so committed to Naomi?** What does this teach us about the power of loyalty and trust in mentorship?
4. **How can we build deep, meaningful relationships across generations?** What are some practical ways to create connections with older or younger women in our lives?

## Real-Life Application

- Think about a younger woman who may need guidance. How can you begin forming a mentoring relationship with her?
- If you are in need of mentorship, pray and ask God to reveal a "Naomi" in your life.

## Action Step

**Identify one woman in your life who could be a mentor or mentee.** Pray about how to nurture that relationship. Consider reaching out to her this week with a message of encouragement, an invitation to coffee, or simply an expression of gratitude.

## A Prayer for Mentorship

**Heavenly Father,**

*Thank You for the gift of intergenerational relationships. I praise You for the wisdom You give through the women who walk before us and for the fresh perspectives from the women coming behind us. Just as You orchestrated the relationship between Naomi and Ruth, I ask You to align me with women who will help me grow in wisdom and faith.*

*Lord, if I am in need of guidance, open my heart to receive instruction. If I am in a position to mentor, let me pour out love, grace, and wisdom in ways that honor You. Remove any fears, insecurities, or hesitations that keep me from engaging in relationships that will bless me and others.*

*May my relationships be rooted in Christ, full of honesty, encouragement, and trust. Let us be women who uplift one another, walking together through life's challenges and victories. I surrender this desire for mentorship to You, Lord, knowing that You will guide my steps.*

*In Jesus' name,*

**Amen.**

# Session 2

## *Walking Through Life's Transitions Together*

### Learning from Naomi and Ruth

**Scripture Focus:**

**Ruth 1:19-22** *(Read aloud or reflect on this passage)*

*"So Naomi returned from Moab accompanied by Ruth the Moabite, her daughter-in-law, arriving in Bethlehem as the barley harvest was beginning."*

— Ruth 1:22 (NIV)

## Key Themes:

- **The Power of Mentorship in Times of Transition:** Naomi and Ruth were both widows facing uncertainty, yet they journeyed together rather than alone.
- **The Role of Vulnerability and Trust:** Naomi was honest about her pain, and Ruth stayed committed to her despite the difficulty.
- **How Mentorship Helps Us Navigate Change:** Mentors provide wisdom, encouragement, and reassurance when we are in transition.

## Connection to *Woman to Woman*

*Chapter 8: A Mentoring Guide* reminds us that mentorship is most impactful during times of transition. Women in their twenties, for example, often struggle with career choices and relationships. Women in their fifties begin thinking about retirement, legacy, and shifting family roles.

Naomi had lived through many seasons of life, giving her the wisdom to help Ruth. The book shares how women of different ages should recognize their own value and seek relationships where they can both receive guidance and pour into others.

In *Chapter 2: Today's Woman in Her Twenties*, a common theme is seeking guidance when navigating uncertainty:

*"Don't feel like you have to figure everything out on your own. Seek counsel from godly women who have walked before you."*

Similarly, Naomi provided Ruth with wisdom for her next steps—guidance that Ruth might not have found on her own.

## Reflection & Discussion Questions

1. **Why do you think Naomi encouraged Ruth to return to her homeland instead of staying with her?** What does this reveal about Naomi's character?
2. **Have you ever gone through a major life transition (loss, career change, relocation, relationship change, etc.)?** How did an older woman help you during that season?
3. **Ruth chose to stay with Naomi despite uncertainty.** What does her loyalty teach us about the importance of steadfast relationships in times of change?
4. **How can we, like Ruth, show loyalty and commitment in mentorship relationships?**
5. **What role does honesty play in mentorship?** Naomi expressed her bitterness and pain. How does transparency impact mentoring relationships today?

## Real-Life Application

- Think about a time when you felt uncertain or lost. Who supported you? What advice did they give that helped you through it?
- If you know someone going through a difficult season, consider reaching out to her this week with encouragement.

## Action Step

**Write a letter (or text) to an older woman who has guided you through a difficult time.** Express gratitude for her wisdom and support, letting her know how much she has impacted your journey.

## A Prayer for Strength in Transition

**Heavenly Father,**

*Thank You for being our ever-present help in times of change. Life brings uncertainty, but You never leave us. Just as You provided Naomi and Ruth with each other during their season of transition, I ask that You surround me with women who will encourage and guide me when I feel uncertain.*

*Lord, help me to be a Ruth—to walk alongside those in need of companionship, wisdom, and support. And help me to be a Naomi—to share my experiences with those who can learn from them. Give me the courage to trust You in every season, knowing that You are working all things for my good.*

*May I be a woman who strengthens others, just as I have been strengthened. Thank You for the relationships that You have placed in my life, and may I never take them for granted.*

*In Jesus' name,*

**Amen.**

# Session 3

## Seeking Wise Counsel

### Learning from Naomi and Ruth

**Scripture Focus:**

> **Ruth 2:1-13** *(Read aloud or reflect on this passage)*
>
> *"She went out, entered a field and began to glean behind the harvesters. As it turned out, she was working in a field belonging to Boaz, who was from the clan of Elimelek."*
>
> — Ruth 2:3 (NIV)

### Key Themes:

- **Naomi as a Guide to Ruth in a New Season of Life:** Naomi helped Ruth navigate unfamiliar territory, just as mentors help younger women transition into new experiences.

- **The Role of Mentors in Providing Wisdom for Major Life Decisions:** Naomi's knowledge helped Ruth make strategic choices about her future.
- **Why Mentees Must Be Humble and Willing to Learn:** Ruth followed Naomi's counsel, showing that a teachable spirit is essential in mentorship.

## Connection to *Woman to Woman*

In *Chapter 8: A Mentoring Guide*, the book highlights the importance of seeking guidance from those who have already walked the path you're on. Naomi had life experience that Ruth lacked, just as older women today carry wisdom that can help younger women avoid unnecessary struggles.

The book reminds us:

*"You can't teach what you don't know."*

Similarly, Naomi didn't try to advise Ruth on everything—she guided her in areas where she had experience. This is a lesson for mentors: Focus on what you know and be honest about what you don't.

Additionally, in *Chapter 4: Today's Woman in Her Forties*, the book discusses the need for seeking wise counsel during transitions:

*"No one has all the answers, and that's okay. The key is knowing where to go for wisdom when you need it."*

Just as Naomi helped Ruth navigate uncertainty, women in every season of life benefit from trusted advisors who offer wisdom, encouragement, and support.

## Reflection & Discussion Questions

1. **Naomi guided Ruth on how to navigate the unfamiliar.** Why is seeking counsel from those with more experience important?
2. **Ruth obeyed Naomi's advice without hesitation.** What can we learn from her willingness to trust?
3. **How do you seek wise counsel in your personal or professional life?** Do you have a mentor or an older woman you turn to for guidance?
4. **What qualities should you look for in a mentor?** What makes someone a reliable and godly source of wisdom?
5. **Have you ever received advice that changed the trajectory of your life?** How did it impact your decision-making?

## Real-Life Application

- Think of an area in your life where you need guidance. Who in your circle might have wisdom in this area? Consider reaching out to her for advice.
- If you are in a position to mentor, ask yourself: What life lessons do I have that could benefit someone younger?

## Action Step

**Identify an area of your life where you need wisdom.** Reach out to a trusted woman this week—whether through a conversation, a phone call, or a meeting—to seek her guidance.

## A Prayer for Wisdom in Mentorship

**Heavenly Father,**

*Thank You for the wisdom You provide through the women You place in our lives. Just as Naomi was a guide to Ruth, I ask that You surround me with wise and godly women who can offer counsel when I need direction. Help me to recognize the mentors You have placed in my life, and give me the humility to seek and receive wisdom.*

*Lord, make me both a receiver and a giver of wisdom. If I am in need of guidance, open my heart to learn from those who have walked before me. If I am in a position to share wisdom, let me do so with grace, humility, and love. Help me to use my experiences to uplift and encourage others.*

*May my relationships be filled with honesty, trust, and a commitment to helping one another grow. Give me discernment in seeking and giving counsel so that I walk in alignment with Your will.*

*In Jesus' name,*

**Amen.**

# Session 4

## *Mentorship in Action*

### Learning from Naomi and Ruth

**Scripture Focus:**

> **Ruth 3:1-11** *(Read aloud or reflect on this passage)*
> "One day Ruth's mother-in-law Naomi said to her, 'My daughter, I must find a home for you, where you will be well provided for.'"
> — Ruth 3:1 (NIV)

### Key Themes:

- **Naomi's Practical Advice to Ruth on Securing Her Future:** Mentorship isn't just about spiritual guidance; it also includes practical, real-world wisdom.

- **The Importance of Mentors Helping Mentees Take Bold Steps:** Naomi encouraged Ruth to step out of her comfort zone and take initiative.
- **The Balance Between Personal Responsibility and Trusting God's Plan:** While Ruth acted on Naomi's advice, she also trusted that God was in control.

### Connection to *Woman to Woman*

In *Chapter 8: A Mentoring Guide*, the book explains that mentors provide clarity and encouragement when their mentees face major decisions. Naomi helped Ruth strategize, teaching us that mentorship includes both encouragement and actionable advice.

The book emphasizes:

*"Mentors don't just tell you what to do; they help you see options and guide you in making wise choices."*

Similarly, in *Chapter 6: Today's Woman in Her Sixties*, women reflect on the importance of passing down wisdom to the next generation:

*"We are called to teach younger women how to navigate life with wisdom and faith. Our experiences are meant to be shared, not hoarded."*

Naomi embraced this responsibility. She didn't just sympathize with Ruth's struggles—she actively helped Ruth take the next step in her journey.

## Reflection & Discussion Questions

1. **Naomi encouraged Ruth to present herself to Boaz with confidence.** Have you ever needed a mentor to push you toward an opportunity?
2. **What is the difference between taking bold action and being impatient?** How do we balance stepping out in faith with waiting on God's timing?
3. **Have you ever felt unsure about a major life decision?** How did guidance from an older woman help you gain clarity?
4. **Naomi didn't just give Ruth advice—she gave her a plan.** Why is it important for mentors to provide both encouragement and practical steps?
5. **Who in your life needs encouragement to take a bold step forward?** How can you be like Naomi to someone in your circle?

## Real-Life Application

- Think of an opportunity where you need to step out in faith but feel hesitant. How can you seek guidance from a mentor to help you take the next step?
- If you are mentoring someone, consider how you can **actively** help her move forward instead of just offering advice.

## Action Step

**Identify an opportunity where you need to step out in faith.** Seek counsel from a mentor and take at least one action toward that opportunity this week.

## A Prayer for Courage in Mentorship

**Heavenly Father,**

*Thank You for the mentors You place in our lives, guiding us through seasons of uncertainty and growth. Just as Naomi provided Ruth with both wisdom and a plan, I ask that You surround me with women who can help me step boldly into my next chapter.*

*Lord, when I feel hesitant or unsure, remind me that You have already equipped me with what I need. Give me the courage to act in faith while trusting in Your perfect timing.*

*If I am in a position to mentor, help me to offer both encouragement and practical wisdom, leading others with grace and humility. May my guidance be rooted in Your truth, and may I point others toward Your purpose for their lives.*

*Let me be bold, wise, and open to the lessons You want me to learn and share.*

*In Jesus' name,*

**Amen.**

# Session 5

## The Rewards of Mentorship

**Learning from Naomi and Ruth**

**Scripture Focus:**

**Ruth 4:13-17** *(Read aloud or reflect on this passage)*

*"The women said to Naomi: 'Praise be to the Lord, who this day has not left you without a guardian-redeemer. May he become famous throughout Israel! He will renew your life and sustain you in your old age. For your daughter-in-law, who loves you and who is better to you than seven sons, has given him birth.'"*

— Ruth 4:14-15 (NIV)

## Key Themes:

- **How Mentorship Blesses Both the Mentor and the Mentee:** Naomi guided Ruth, and in return, Ruth's faithfulness brought Naomi renewed joy and purpose.
- **The Legacy of Intergenerational Wisdom:** The relationship between Naomi and Ruth impacted future generations, ultimately leading to the lineage of Jesus Christ.
- **How Investing in Others Creates a Lasting Impact:** Mentorship is not just for today—it has the power to influence the future.

## Connection to *Woman to Woman*

In *Chapter 8: A Mentoring Guide*, the book highlights that **mentorship is a two-way street**—both the mentor and mentee benefit from the relationship. Naomi helped Ruth navigate life, but in the end, Ruth provided Naomi with a new sense of purpose and joy.

The book states:

*"When you pour into someone else, God often uses that relationship to bless you in return."*

Similarly, in *Chapter 5: Today's Woman in Her Fifties*, the book discusses how **mentorship is about leaving a legacy**:

*"As we grow older, it's not just about what we achieve but about who we help along the way. Our wisdom is meant to outlive us."*

Naomi's guidance didn't just change Ruth's life—it shaped **generations to come**.

## Reflection & Discussion Questions

1. **How did Ruth's faithfulness bless Naomi in the end?** What does this teach us about the long-term rewards of mentorship?
2. **What is the role of mentorship in leaving a lasting legacy?** How has guidance from another woman shaped your journey?
3. **Have you ever been blessed unexpectedly through a mentoring relationship?** How did that experience impact you?
4. **Naomi's mentorship played a role in God's greater plan.** How can we be intentional about passing down wisdom to future generations?
5. **What is one way you can be a mentor to someone younger?** How can you start investing in her today?

## Real-Life Application

- Reflect on a time when someone's guidance made a significant impact on your life. How can you now offer that same wisdom to someone else?
- Consider a young woman in your family, church, or workplace who could benefit from mentorship. What steps can you take to pour into her life?

## Action Steps

**Review the case study in the appendix.** Answer the questions and consider how you might leverage the lessons.

**Make a plan for how you will mentor or seek mentorship in the next year.** Write down the names of women you can learn from or pour into, and take the first step toward building those relationships.

## A Prayer for Lasting Impact in Mentorship

**Heavenly Father,**

*Thank You for the power of mentorship and the relationships that shape our journeys. Just as Naomi and Ruth's bond had generational significance, help me to invest in relationships that leave a lasting impact.*

*Lord, open my heart to both receive and give wisdom. If I am in need of guidance, lead me to godly women who will help me grow. If I have wisdom to share, give me the courage and willingness to pour into others with love and patience.*

*Help me to see the value of mentorship not just in my own life but in the more remarkable story You are writing. Let my relationships be purposeful, my words be encouraging, and my legacy be one of faith and wisdom.*

*In Jesus' name,*

**Amen.**

# Session 6

## Becoming Women Who Lift as We Rise

**Reflecting on the Journey of Mentorship**

Throughout this study, we have seen the power of intergenerational mentorship through the story of Naomi and Ruth. Their journey reveals the impact of godly wisdom, trust, and commitment in relationships between women.

From Naomi's willingness to guide Ruth to Ruth's faithful obedience, we learn that mentorship is not just about instruction—it is about walking alongside someone in faith. It is about pouring into others with intention, receiving wisdom with humility, and trusting that God uses our relationships to shape His greater plan.

## Key Takeaways from Each Session

1. **The Power of Relationship (Ruth 1:1-18)**
   - Mentorship starts with **connection** and **trust**.
   - Relationships across generations can provide **wisdom, strength, and encouragement**.
   - **Action Step:** Identify a mentor or mentee and start nurturing that relationship.

2. **Walking Through Life's Transitions Together (Ruth 1:19-22)**
   - Life's **transitions** are more manageable when we have wise women guiding us.
   - Mentorship thrives in seasons of **change and uncertainty**.
   - **Action Step:** Write a note of gratitude to an older woman who has helped you through a transition.

3. **Seeking Wise Counsel (Ruth 2:1-13)**
   - Wise counsel helps us make **godly, strategic decisions**.
   - A teachable spirit is essential in every mentoring relationship.
   - **Action Step:** Seek guidance from a trusted mentor on an important decision.

4. **Mentorship in Action (Ruth 3:1-11)**
   - Mentors help mentees **take bold steps** toward their God-given purpose.
   - A great mentor doesn't just **offer advice**—she provides a **plan**.
   - **Action Step:** Take one bold step toward an opportunity where you need faith.

5. **The Rewards of Mentorship (Ruth 4:13-17)**
   - **Mentorship is a two-way street**—both mentor and mentee are blessed.
   - Investing in others **leaves a legacy** beyond our lifetime.

- **Action Step:** Make a plan to mentor or seek mentorship in the next year.

## How Naomi and Ruth Exemplify Mentorship

The story of Naomi and Ruth (Ruth 1-4) is a powerful model of mentorship, loyalty, and wisdom between two women from different generations.

Naomi, an older widow, had walked through grief, change, and hardship. Ruth, a younger widow, faced uncertainty about her future. Despite their differences, they chose to journey together—learning from and supporting each other.

What Naomi's Mentorship Teaches Us:

- **She was a source of wisdom.** Naomi guided Ruth in making wise decisions about her future.
- **She cared for Ruth's well-being.** Naomi didn't just give advice; she helped Ruth navigate life's transitions.
- **She encouraged bold action.** Naomi pushed Ruth to take courageous steps toward God's provision.

What Ruth's Teachable Spirit Teaches Us:

- **She was willing to learn.** Ruth trusted Naomi's wisdom and followed her guidance.
- **She remained loyal.** Even when Naomi encouraged her to go back home, Ruth stayed committed.
- **She took action.** Ruth stepped out in faith, embracing new opportunities based on Naomi's counsel.

Their mentorship was mutual—Naomi poured into Ruth's life, but Ruth's loyalty and love also renewed Naomi's hope.

Every woman can benefit from having both a mentor and a mentee. Just as Naomi and Ruth walked together, this study guide encourages us to build relationships where we learn from and invest in each other.

## Final Reflection & Commitment to Mentorship

Naomi's mentorship of Ruth was not just about helping her find security; it was about shaping a future that would ultimately be part of God's redemptive plan. This story is a reminder that when women pour into one another, we are part of something bigger than ourselves.

No matter what season of life you are in, you have a role to play:

- **If you are a Ruth**, be **open to wisdom**, willing to learn, and faithful in your relationships.
- **If you are a Naomi**, take **responsibility for sharing your experiences**, offering encouragement, and guiding with love.

God calls us to **lift as we rise**—to **support, encourage, and invest in one another**. This is the essence of intergenerational mentorship.

## Call to Action: Who Will You Pour Into?

- **If you need a mentor:** Pray for guidance and be intentional about seeking wisdom from an older woman.
- **If you are in a position to mentor:** Look for younger women in your church, workplace, family, or community who need encouragement and wisdom.
- **If you are both a mentor and a mentee (as many of us are!):** Commit to both seeking and giving wisdom—being a bridge between generations.

Take a moment to reflect:

1. Who is one woman I can reach out to this week for mentorship or guidance?
2. Who is one younger woman I can **pour into** this month?

Make a commitment today. **Write their names down, pray over them, and take the first step.**

# A Closing Prayer for Mentorship & Legacy

**Heavenly Father,**

*Thank You for the gift of mentorship and for the women You place in our lives to guide, uplift, and encourage us. Just as You used Naomi and Ruth to bless one another and impact future generations, I pray that You help me be intentional in my relationships with other women.*

*If I need guidance, lead me to godly mentors who will speak truth and wisdom into my life. Give me a teachable spirit so I may receive counsel with humility.*

*If I am in a position to mentor, help me to do so with grace, patience, and love. Let my words be seasoned with wisdom, and may my actions reflect the love of Christ.*

*Lord, I surrender my relationships to You. May they be purposeful, life-giving, and transformative. Use me to leave a legacy of faith, wisdom, and encouragement for the women coming behind me.*

*In Jesus' name,*

**Amen.**

## Final Words

## *You Are Part of God's Greater Story*

*M*entorship is not just about offering advice—it is about building relationships that reflect God's love. When women support one another, we create a legacy of wisdom, faith, and empowerment that ripples through generations.

This is your invitation to step boldly into mentorship. Whether you are a Ruth seeking guidance or a Naomi offering wisdom, you are part of God's greater story.

Go forth, build meaningful relationships, and lift as you rise.

# Appendix
## Intergenerational Mentoring Case Study

Tasha Holmes was nervous as she entered the convention center's bustling room for a women's leadership event. At 33, she was proud of her career accomplishments but felt overwhelmed by the pressure of balancing professional growth with her personal life and the nagging sense that she wasn't quite measuring up. A particular speaker caught her attention during the Q&A session of a panel discussion on *Getting the Life You Want*. At 58, Denise McCoy was striking with naturally curly hair, perfect makeup, and a beautiful red knit suit. She spoke with calm confidence, sharing her journey of transitioning from a high-powered corporate role to a purpose-driven semi-retired life focused on mentoring and community service. Her words resonated deeply with Tasha, who was drawn to Denise's poise and wisdom.

After the session, Tasha waited in line to speak with her. "Thank you for sharing your story," she began, her voice slightly shaky, "I'm navigating some challenges at work and was really inspired by your advice on finding balance. Do you have any tips for advocating for yourself without coming across as difficult?"

Denise smiled warmly, sensing Tasha's nervousness and genuine desire to learn. "It's all about being clear and confident in your value," she replied. They spoke for a few minutes more, and Tasha shared more context regarding her job and how she hoped to get into a management role. Denise admired Tasha's curiosity, ambition, and openness to growth. She also saw something of herself in how Tasha had courageously moved away from home after graduating from college to follow her dreams. "Why don't we meet for coffee next week and talk more?" Tasha agreed eagerly, and their mentoring journey began.

Over the next several months, they met at a cozy café, where their conversations ranged from career strategies to personal growth and relationships. Denise enjoyed their conversations but noticed that Tasha tended to wear clothes that didn't complement her shape and size. She decided to pray for an opportunity to speak to her about it. In the meantime, Tasha opened up about a recent challenge at work: her supervisor had taken credit for a successful marketing campaign she had spearheaded. "I'm frustrated, but I don't know how to address it without jeopardizing my reputation and maybe even my career," she admitted.

Denise listened carefully before offering her insight. "I've been there," she said, leaning in. "I've learned that you have to advocate for yourself. But you can do it with grace. Why don't we role-play the conversation?"

Over the next hour, Denise helped Tasha craft a message that was both assertive and professional. She encouraged Tasha to say, "I'd like to clarify my contributions to ensure transparency," rather than confronting her supervisor aggressively. "And before you go in, I'd like to suggest that you pray for wisdom and guidance," Denise added, " There is a scripture in Proverbs 3:5-6 which says, 'Trust in the Lord with all your heart and lean not on your own understanding.' I've always found this helpful to meditate on when I wasn't feeling confident."

The conversation with her supervisor was as nerve-wracking as she feared, but Tasha emerged stronger for speaking up for herself. Her supervisor acknowledged her contributions, and her team's respect for her grew. "It worked!" Tasha told Denise during their next meeting, "I felt like I finally found my voice." She beamed with pride as she slid into the chair across the table. The outfit Tasha wore was trendy but not very flattering. Denise wondered if this was something she wore to work.

Denise decided this was an opportunity to speak up regarding professional attire. She whispered a quick prayer and said, "Tasha, it's great that you've learned to advocate for yourself. If you want to move up, you must also focus on looking the part. I've noticed that your clothes don't always fit properly. One tip that my mother taught me is that a polished look always starts with a good foundation."

Tasha looked confused, "What do you mean by foundation?"

"The old folks just to jokingly say 'it must be jelly, cause jam don't shake like that' when a woman didn't have on a girdle. The foundation is your underwear. You don't have to spend a lot of money on clothes, but every woman should invest in a good bra and support garments for a smooth, polished look. It's really important that you look pulled together and professional if you want them to see you as having management potential. If you have some time today, I'd be happy to go shopping with you and show you the brands I like."

"Wow! That would be amazing. I've always just bought underwear from discount stores based on what fit. If you don't mind, I'd love for us to go shopping together."

"Mind? Girl, that's one of my favorite things to do."

Beyond professional guidance, their relationship began to delve into all aspects of personal and spiritual growth. Denise often shared how her faith had guided her through life's challenges, including navigating loss and career transitions. One day, as they discussed self-doubt, Denise opened up about her own struggles. "I used to beat myself up over mistakes," she confessed, "But an older woman I admired once told me to forgive myself because no one expected me to be perfect. That helped me and taught me to focus on learning from my mistakes."

Tasha, who had long wrestled with feelings of inadequacy, was tearing up. "I've never thought about it that way," she said. Inspired by Denise's vulnerability, she began journaling about the times she needed to extend grace to herself.

Their faith became a central thread in their conversations. They often ended their meetings with prayer, thanking God for their growth and seeking His guidance for what lay ahead. Denise introduced Tasha to scripture-based affirmations, encouraging her to speak truths like "I am fearfully and wonderfully made" over her life.

As their mentoring relationship evolved, Denise realized Tasha was also teaching her. "You've reignited my passion for helping others," Denise told her one day. Encouraged by Tasha's fresh perspective, Denise began volunteering at her church, mentoring young professionals in her community. "Sometimes younger women remind us of where we've been and show us how much we still have to give," she reflected.

Tasha, in turn, began to thrive both professionally and personally. She got promoted at work and started leading a Bible study for young women at her church. "I never would have had the confidence to do this without you," she told Denise, "You've helped me see myself the way God sees me."

Their bond, rooted in shared faith, mutual respect, and a genuine desire to see each other grow, became a source of strength for both women. Tasha often marveled at how a single conversation at a leadership event had transformed her life. And Denise felt grateful for the chance to pour into a younger woman's journey while reigniting her own sense of purpose.

## Discussion Questions

1. How did Denise's combination of practical advice and spiritual guidance impact Tasha's personal and professional growth?
2. What role did vulnerability play in building trust and strengthening their relationship?
3. How did their shared faith shape the mentoring dynamic and their individual growth?
4. In what ways did Tasha's presence inspire Denise to rediscover her purpose?
5. How can this story encourage others to seek or offer mentoring relationships that blend professional, personal, and spiritual elements?

www.ingramcontent.com/pod-product-compliance
Lightning Source LLC
LaVergne TN
LVHW041716060526
838201LV00043B/770